21 Life Applicable
Revelations from God's Word

21 Life Applicable Revelations from God's Word

"Thus speaketh the LORD God of Israel, saying, Write thee all the words that I have spoken unto thee in a book" [Jeremiah 30:2]
Volume 1

Anthony Adefarakan

GLOEM, CANADA

CONTENTS

Introduction   1

#One   3

#Two   5

#Three   7

#Four   11

#Five   13

#Six   17

#Seven   19

#Eight   21

#Nine   23

#Ten   25

#Eleven   27

#Twelve   29

CONTENTS

#Thirteen 31

#Fourteen 35

#Fifteen 37

#Sixteen 41

#Seventeen 45

#Eighteen 49

#Nineteen 53

#Twenty 55

#Twenty One 57

Become a Financial Partner with Jesus 59

About the Author 61

Introduction

Life on earth has been described as a form of pilgrimage (1 Peter 2:11, Hebrews 11:13) with eternity as man's final destination.

In the course of this brief earthly sojourn, man is bound to face certain situations capable of generating questions like *'what step do I take?' 'where do I settle?' 'who do I marry?' 'will I be rich or poor?' 'how do I finance my projects?' 'how do I take good care of my family?' 'how do I know God's will for my life?'* just to mention a few. Usually, men find it difficult to provide correct answers to these questions due to their weak mortal nature.

However, there is a manual for this pilgrimage, which is the Word of God. The One Who designed this journey for man has put in the manual all he needs to navigate his way successfully and to eventually end up on the glorious side of eternity when the pilgrimage is over. Little wonder David prayed in Psalm 119:19 – *"I am a stranger in the earth; hide not thy commandment from me".*

In this Holy Spirit inspired book, the Lord will be opening your eyes to certain revelations from His Word, capable of providing answers to the questions on your mind and pointing you in the right path to take in order to experience a fulfilled life here on earth and to attain a glorious eternity when the journey is over.

Deuteronomy 29:29 says *"The secret things belong unto the LORD, our God; but those things which are revealed belong unto us and to our children forever, that we may do all the words of this law".* As you encounter the secret things which the Lord has revealed by His Spirit in this book, determine to prayerfully apply them in your life and situations; you will record unusual testimonies and God's light will shine upon your ways – Job 22:28, Psalm 119:105.

ANTHONY ADEFARAKAN

Be blessed as you read on.

#One

Revelation 4:6-8 (AKJV)

'And before the throne there was a sea of glass...and round about the throne were four beasts full of eyes before and behind. And the first beast was like a lion, and the second beast like a calf, and the third beast had a face as a man, and the fourth beast was like a flying eagle ...and they were full of eyes within: and they rest not day and night, saying, Holy, holy, holy, Lord God Almighty, which was, and is, and is to come."

Application:

Consider the appearances of the four living creatures according to verses 7 and 8;

By implication, all men – those in authority, babies, happy ones, unhappy ones, the highly placed, the aged etc –must constantly offer God glory, honour and thanks (Revelation 4:9).

Furthermore, it is worthy of note that those creatures were 'living creatures' and they were 'four' in number. This tells us that God only expects praise and worship from living beings; and wherever such living beings are located –whether in the North, South, East or West – He demands their worship. Being four in number means God expects praises and worship from the four winds of the earth. So as long as you live, regardless of your location on the surface of the earth, you must worship Him.[Psalm 34:1, 104:33, 115:17, 118:17, Isaiah 38:18-19].

Still considering these living creatures, the Bible says they were full of eyes in front, at the back and within [Revelation 4:6, 8]. Why were they full of eyes and not nose, ears or some other organs? It is because you need the ability to see reasons in order to worship God effectively. If you engage the eyes behind you, you will be able to see your past. And with that you will see reasons to worship God. If you look ahead of you, you will see your future, and that will help you to worship Him some more. Then if you look within you, that is, if you look inward you will discover that God really deserves your worship. That is why the Psalmist says in Psalm 103:1 'Bless the Lord, oh my soul; and all that is within me, bless His holy name'. He looked within and saw reasons why God should be praised. Whenever you look back, ahead or within, you will definitely see reasons God should be worshipped.

Action: Go ahead and worship Him from the depth of your heart.

#Two

Proverbs 4:7 [ERV]

'Wisdom begins when you decide to get wisdom. So use everything you own to get wisdom! [Then you will become wise]'

Application:
The 'decision' to get anything is what initiates the process of getting that very thing. And to eventually get it, you must be willing to pay the price by 'using' or 'engaging' what you already have. That is, every desire that will manifest must attract some level of self-denial or sacrifice. A price must be paid and good enough everyone can afford the price –it is simply 'using everything you own'.

For instance, in Mark 5:25-34, the woman with the issue of blood decided to get her healing and she took corresponding steps to get her desire fulfilled. The process of her healing was initiated when she 'decided to go' and it was complete when she paid the price of pushing her way through to Jesus to do what she planned doing.

She simply used what she owned –her hands, her eyes, her legs, her fingers etc.

This principle does not just work in getting wisdom, it works in getting other desires of yours fulfilled. Just follow the steps and you will have your desires granted.

1. Decide on what you want- be clear about it.
2. Look at the things you already own; the resources at your disposal [not necessarily money]. Identify them [without underestimating any of them].

3. Then, engage them fully towards the actualization of your desire. You will surely get it.

Action: What do you want? Name it on a sheet of paper (just an item please, not two). Follow the steps listed above – think outside the box and pay the price. Once you get your desire, give thanks to God and go for another desire until your joy is full [John 16:24, Psalm 37:4].

#Three

2 Corinthians 2: 14-16 [AKJV]

'Now thanks be unto God, which always causeth us to triumph in Christ and maketh manifest the savour of His knowledge by us in every place. For we are unto God a sweet savour of Christ, in them that are saved, and in them that perish: To the one we are the savour of death unto death; and to the other the savour of life unto life...'

Application:

Verse 14 of that scripture starts with the word 'Now' - meaning regardless of the blows the devil had dealt you in times past, regardless of the number of times you have failed and have been embarrassed, you can boldly say 'thanks be to God' because 'Now', things will be different. Isaiah 43:18-19 says you should not remember the former things nor consider the things of old because God is doing a new thing. Hallelujah!

The second part of that same verse 14 says 'and maketh manifest the savour of His knowledge by us in every place'. This is deep! It means the knowledge of God has savour (perfume, aroma, fragrance) and therefore can be perceived. There is an aroma proceeding from a believer who carries the knowledge of God, and the aroma does two things to people when perceived – it gives life to those who need to be saved and gives death to those who should die – 2Corinthians 2:15-16. For instance in the natural, you may perceive the aroma of a particular perfume worn by someone and simply derive pleasure from it, while to another person, especially people with respiratory disorders, the same aroma (particularly when in high intensity) may cause discomfort and could even trigger a crisis. In the same way, a person with respiratory disorder will avoid contact with such a fellow, so also will demons and other agents of darkness keep off your territory. Not because they are afraid of you or your prayers, but because you possess the aroma (fragrance) of God's knowledge. The devil knows those who know God. Notice the last part of verse 14 says '...in every place'. That means, this wonder is not location specific. It happens everywhere. It therefore follows that wherever you go with the knowledge of God in you, your victory is always guaranteed.

The knowledge of God simply means **'what you know about God'**. So, whenever you are faced with any problematic situation, the first thing to do is not to pray but to find out what God has said concerning the matter. Be it barrenness, poverty, sickness, diseases, death etc, there is at least one knowledge of God you can possess about each of these situations; and when you start searching the scriptures for it, the 'perfume' is already being applied. The moment you locate your word you will know, and the aroma of that revelation when applied in prayer will drive the devil away from your territory. When that happens, you are said to have been delivered. Don't pray until you have discovered a particular knowledge of God to hang your prayers on. The answers come faster and quicker that way. Even the devil knows that. And good enough, this doesn't have to be on a mountain or in the church; the Bible says 'in every place' –including villages, towns, cities, overseas etc. Perfume diffuses in every place.

Also, notice that the Bible didn't say occasionally, sometimes, many times, or even almost every time; rather, it says 'ALWAYS'. So, with this perfume of God's knowledge at work, your constant victory (triumph) is guaranteed.

However, Apostle Paul didn't forget to point out that this triumph can only be experienced 'in Christ' (verse 14), and not in skill, academic degree, nor in political connection. It must be 'in Christ'. Thus, being in Christ is the first step to take before this divine perfume can begin to work for you. You have to be washed and cleansed in the Blood of Jesus before applying the perfume. If you don't, your filthy smell of sin will render the effect of the perfume useless and as such, you will not be able to experience the triumph the perfume brings. Give your life to Christ now; be born again and your triumph will be guaranteed!

Action: The source of all the needed knowledge of God for your triumph is the Bible – The Word of God. Grab a copy, search the contents and you will locate your own word (perfume) there. Victory is yours!

#Four

2 Corinthians 6:10c [TLB]

'We own nothing, and yet we enjoy everything...'

Application:

As a Christian, you really own nothing. Whatever the Lord gives you or releases in your direction belongs to Him. He only gives them to you to enjoy. 1 Corinthians 10:26 says '...the earth and every good thing in it belongs to the Lord and is yours to enjoy'. That shows God alone is the owner of all things; man only possesses them at one time or the other. This mindset should help you never to hold on too tightly to anything you possess here on earth. If God (the Owner of all things) decides to ask you for any of the things He has given you to enjoy, you are expected to quickly give it to Him, and even appreciate Him for allowing you to enjoy it in the first place. John 3:27 says a man has nothing except he be given from above. Job 1:21 also confirms this.

Action: Don't hold on to anything; only enjoy it with a sense of gratitude to the Owner. Never forget that.

#Five

2 Corinthians 1: 22 [TLB]

'He has put his brand upon us – his mark of ownership – and given us his Holy spirit in our hearts as guarantee that we belong to Him, and as the first installment of all that He is going to give us"

Application:

A brand literally means a mark of identification, especially to distinguish some things from other things having similar nature or features.

For instance, there are many cell phones in the market, but branding is what helps us to know which is which. One cannot just get to the market and say 'I need a cell phone'; the question such a fellow will likely be asked is 'which type?' And that is another way of asking 'which brand?'

Now, the one who does the branding has certain purposes in mind which either are directly or indirectly being communicated to others. A product carrying a brand implies among others the following;

1. This product is the property of the One whose brand it carries. A mark of ownership is on it.
2. The product is distinguished from all other products in existence even if they have the same colour or show close similarities. The brand stands it out from all others.
3. The product cannot get lost in the market (crowd), it is easily identified by its brand name.

4. The ownership of the product cannot be claimed by any other person. No one can claim ownership of another man's branded product.
5. The owner is fully aware of the location of the product. He knows where they are.
6. The owner may decide to withdraw the branded product from the market (unto himself). The owner can stop the product's circulation in the market. He has the final say over the products carrying his brand name.

In the same way, God has marked all His children with the 'brand' or 'seal' of the Holy Spirit and He's confident that though we are in the world, we are not of the world –John 17:14. By the Holy Spirit given to us as a brand, we are clearly noted and distinguished everywhere as God's own – though we may look like every other person in appearance.

No power or principality can claim us because our mark is clear enough; and when Jesus Christ shall return, He will gather to His Father everyone with this brand of the Holy Spirit. Once He sees this brand on you, He will rapture you.

Now you have a responsibility; ensure you remain branded for Christ, don't try to look like other brands so as not to suffer the consequences of mistaken identity. The brand must remain clear and evident on you till Christ returns.

It can also be seen this way, the Holy Spirit we are branded with represents a seal or stamp on us –like a letter being posted to a particular location. No one has the legal right to access the content of the letter except the rightful recipient of the letter at the specified location. So also, as God's children we are being posted to eternity to be with God (with our stamp as the seal of our redemption) – the Holy Spirit. No devil is therefore legally permitted to tamper with us until we finally arrive at our destination where our Father is (in Heaven) –Ephesians 4:30.

Action:

Get branded and remain branded for Christ until you see your Father in glory. Receive the Holy Spirit.

#Six

Mark 11: 22-23 [AKJV]

'And Jesus answering saith unto them; Have faith in God. For verily I say unto you: That whosoever shall say unto this mountain, Be thou removed, and be thou cast into the sea; and shall not doubt in his heart, but shall believe that those things which he saith shall come to pass; he shall have whatsoever he saith."

Application:

There is a life applicable mathematical equation derivable from this scripture – it is called the "equation of faith".

Given that $X = A$, and X is $a + b + c$

It therefore means that $a + b + c = A$

From the text,

X = Have faith in God

a = Issue a command

b = Do not doubt that command (in your heart)

c = Believe that the command will come to pass

A = Experience the result (outcome) of your command.

As a believer, to have faith in God means to declare what you want (issue a command), ensure you don't doubt the declaration in your heart, and believe (with expectation) that the result (outcome) of the declaration shall manifest. With the application of this formula, the result shall manifest (you shall have whatsoever you have said) –verse 23.

Note however, the variable 'a' in this equation can be any command or desire as long as it doesn't contradict God's Word.

Action:

Stop complaining and start declaring your expectations.

#Seven

Matthew 19: 26c, Mark 9:23 [AKJV]

'But with God all things are possible';
'Jesus said unto him, If thou canst believe, all things are possible to him that believeth.'

Application:
From these scriptures, a mathematical formula can be derived.
a = c and
b = c
Therefore, 'a' must be equal to 'b' since they are both equal to 'c'.
That is, if **a = c** and **b = c**, then **a = b**
Where a = God
b = Believer
c = All things are possible
It means with God all things are possible and with a believer (in God), all things are also possible. By inference, a believer is equal to God in this regard because their results are the same.

Psalm 82:6 says 'ye are gods' as well as in John 10:34-35. Also, John 10:30 says 'I and my Father are one'. The moment you begin to exercise faith –believing the Word of God without reservations, you become translated into the realm of God; and you literally begin to record God-kind of results. That is, you start doing what God can do. Jesus said so, and one of His names is 'The Truth' –John 14:6.

Action:

Without faith, you are a mere man; but with your faith in operation, you are a god. Choose where you belong, the invitation is open to all.

#Eight

Philippians 4: 8 [AKJV]

'Finally, brethren, whatsoever things are true, whatsoever things are honest, whatsoever things are just, whatsoever things are pure, whatsoever things are lovely, whatsoever things of good report; if there be any virtue, and if there be any praise, think on these things."

Application:

On the 28th day of January, 2011 at about 8:20pm, a text message from one of the mobile phone companies came into my phone which I deleted instantly because I didn't need the information it contained. Just at that moment, it dawned on me that I have the power to dictate the content(s) of my phone's mail box.

Anyone anywhere can at any time send a mail or text message to your system or phone, but you, the owner of the system or phone, dictate which of them stays in your mail box and which one gets deleted.

All the information in your mail box are those you chose to retain. You know about them.

In the same manner Satan, demons, friends, families, coworkers, neighbours – in fact, anyone anywhere at any point in time may say what they like to you (either positive or negative); they are very free. But it is your sole responsibility to decide which one stays in your mind or gets discarded.

No one can force any negative thing or thought on you. You always have a choice on what to dwell upon –Philippians 4:8.

Action:

You can choose your thoughts the same way you choose your clothes. If a particular thought is unfavourable, simply delete it and move on. You may have no power to stop thoughts from coming at you, but you surely have the power to dictate which one stays with you or not.

#Nine

Luke 11:52 [AKJV]

'Woe unto you, lawyers! for ye have taken away the key of knowledge: ye entered not in yourselves, and them that were entering in ye hindered".

Application:

Jesus Christ in the verse above described knowledge as a key. To fully understand the import of this truth, it is imperative that we analyze the functions of a key, which in itself has been defined by a dictionary as 'something that affords a means of access; something that secures or controls entrance to a place or something that affords a means of clarifying a problem'.

A key locks and unlocks doors thereby granting access as well as denying access to a place. A key is an instrument of control and confers confidence in the one who possesses it.

Now Jesus was saying in effect that knowledge is what determines a man's access into any door he desires to walk through.

To open up a locked door in a man's life, knowledge is the key; and to lock up an unwanted door, knowledge is also required.

Furthermore, to gain control over any situation in life knowledge is required. In other words, it is what a man knows that determines the doors that will be opened to him or locked against him. And this knowledge is not the common sense knowledge but the knowledge that comes from God's Word through revelation. This is because everything in existence has its root in God's Word – nothing was created without the Word –John 1:1-3, Hebrews 11:3.

Action:

What do you want to access in life? Get into the Word to pick up the required key. What door do you want to lock up in your life? Pick the key in the Word. God's Word provides you with the key of knowledge which puts you in control of circumstances (Matthew 16:13-19, Revelation 3:7-8). To get this key however, you will have to learn to meditate on God's Word until the key drops.

#Ten

John 8: 32 [KJV]

'And ye shall know the truth, and the truth shall make you free'

Application:

According to this scripture, it is a settled matter that it takes the truth to make free. Nothing can be done against the truth but for the truth (2Corinthians 13:8). But as powerful as the truth in its ability to set free is, it can't set anyone free until it is discovered (known). Anyone who desires the freedom the truth gives will first have to establish a relationship with it through knowledge.

The key to this relationship is found in John 8:31 where Jesus said to know the truth will involve continuing in His Word which itself is the truth (John 17:17).

Once you get to know the truth (God's Word), no bondage can survive in your life again. But until then you can't enjoy the freedom it offers.

Action:

The truth sets free any day, anywhere and anytime; there is no controversy about that. However, to partake of this freedom, you will have to continue in God's Word in order to possess the revelation knowledge of the truth. Remember, it is the truth that you know that will set you free, not the one others think you know by reason of your spiritual level or church title.

#Eleven

Mark 11:14 [KJV]

'And Jesus answered and said unto it, No man eat fruit of thee hereafter for ever. And His disciples heard it'

Application:

The scripture above says '...Jesus answered'. This means that fig tree referred to in verse 13 was saying something to Jesus. It was speaking disappointment, hunger, deception (with leaves), and even wasted energy and effort because Jesus had to walk to it (so energy must have been dissipated). It was practically challenging the Person and authority of Jesus; that's why He had to answer by laying a curse on it.

How does this affect you as a child of God? The challenges facing you are actually saying something, and you don't need to call on Pastors in order to answer them. Use your own mouth to declare what you want to happen to the situation; and just like the fig tree obeyed Jesus, it will obey you too – Mark 11:20-21.

Note that Jesus clearly uttered what He wanted, to the extent that His disciples heard it. He didn't murmur it, it wasn't a silent declaration, and neither was He thinking about it in His heart. He spoke so loudly that the root of the tree heard (despite its distance in the ground); and the result was just as He said it. He had what he said (Mark 11:23).

As a believer, not making your confessions audibly enough is a sign of doubt; if you are sure of what you are saying, you will say it aloud for anyone who cares to hear. You've got to let your headache, cancer, poverty and other situations you want changed hear your voice. Jesus said in verse 23; 'whoso ever shall say' not whosoever shall think, feel, complain, grumble, murmur, tell Pastor to say or beg - none of these. But whosoever shall SAY. You must learn to always SAY boldly, clearly and confidently what you believe – especially the rooted knowledge you have been able to discover in God's Word. With this understanding, you are never to say what you don't want to have, because Jesus concluded by saying – 'he shall have whatsoever he saith' – verse 23. Watch your tongue; and only say what you want to see. God called for light and what He saw was light – Genesis 1: 3-4.

Now, a quick lesson from the curse Jesus placed on the fig tree. The curse implies that whatsoever (fruit) you cannot offer or give to God, you will never be able to give to any other'. For example, if you refuse to give your life to Christ, you will surely lose it; no man, including you, shall be able to have it.

If you refuse to offer your substance or property to Christ, you will surely lose it. No man, including you, shall be able to have it. But whatever you give to Him, He preserves and establishes in a multiplied form – John 15:2. The Rule is – 'Deny Christ fruits and you may never be fruitful again'.

Remember, though Isaac was offered, he was retained – Genesis 22:9-13.

Action:

Whether you are faced with challenges of human or non-human origin, your words can determine their fate. Use your mouth!

#Twelve

Romans 4:17-18 [AKJV]

'(As it is written, I have made thee a father of nations,) before Him whom he believed, even God, Who quickeneth the dead, and calleth those things which be not as though they were. Who against hope believed in hope, that he might become the father of many nations, according to that which was spoken, So shall thy seed be".

Application:

There is what God has made you, but there's what you must do to become that which has been said or written concerning you. God said He had made Abram a father of many nations, and to show him how serious He was, He gave him a new name which agreed with what He had made him – Abraham, which means 'father of many nations'; that is the meaning of 'calling those things which be not as though they were'. However, for Abraham to become that which was spoken concerning him, he had the responsibility of believing in hope against hope; disregarding his dead body and his wife, Sarah's dead womb – which were real in the physical. He held on to that which was spoken by God as against what was obviously and evidently happening to him and his wife. He didn't deny the deadness, he only disregarded (ignored) it. He counted it immaterial compared to God's declaration.

Because of this (as recorded in detail in verses 19-21), he finally and eventually became 'the father of many nations' –even though it took 25 years from the time he was promised.

In effect, Abram was already bearing Abraham before he actually became Abraham –verse 17. That means, a sister can start bearing her husband's name in faith before she even meets him. Also, a brother may start making pledges in his and his wife's name before the actual marriage. You may start answering names you wish to bear or one may even start calling a barren woman by her children's names in faith. Furthermore, one could start saying 'how was work today?' to the unemployed, and you could even start behaving like a car owner or landlord when none of them is yet visible.

Nothing is too big for God to accomplish. Just find out what He has said concerning you through dreams, prophecies, His Word or other channels He uses to communicate His will to you. Believe it wholeheartedly and start calling yourself, describing yourself and even seeing yourself like that; disregarding the events or happenings around you which are contrary to your WORD as declared by God. Just be giving glory to God –verse 20, and keep rejoicing in hope –Romans 12:12. Before long, it will manifest.

Note this as well, to become the king God said He has made you according to Revelation 5:10, you need to start seeing yourself as one.

Action:
Choose to disregard/ignore every form of evidence in and around your life which are contrary to your expectations from God. Be totally focused on God's promises that you literally lose sight of any contrary sign. That is what Abraham did before his Isaac could manifest. Now you know, do same (John 13:17).

#Thirteen

Mark 5:35-42 [AKJV]

'...And when he was come in, he saith unto them, why make ye this ado, and weep? the damsel is not dead, but sleepeth...'

Application:

In raising Jairus' daughter, Jesus first converted 'death' to 'sleep' by His Words. He did this before telling the girl to get up; and she did. He didn't have to pray about it.

Also concerning Lazarus in John 11:1-44, He said our friend Lazarus sleepeth, let us go and wake him up. When He arrived, he gave thanks for the sake of the people around and thereafter, he just called him forth at once.

In Acts 9:36-41, Peter didn't say Dorcas was asleep but agreed that she was dead. That's why he needed to really pray before she came back to life.

The secret of Jesus was in what He said before attending to the situation. The moment He said it was not death but sleep, the spirit of death left her and the situation was naturally converted to sleep. So, with the assurance of what had happened, all He needed to do was just to wake her up from her sleep. In the natural, when someone is sleeping, you don't need to pray before the fellow gets up; all you need do is wake him up –either by calling or touching. Jesus called lazarus but touched Jairus' daughter. Even when He (the Lord) was sleeping in the boat, His disciples didn't pray for Him to get up; rather they simply woke Him up.

As a Christian, you must learn to apply this principle of calling forth what you want to see before addressing a situation. If you don't, you will have to pray more like Peter did before Dorcas could be raised back to life.

Use your mouth to convert situations to your advantage; don't agree with what you don't desire to experience. Change it by your words.

Note this, when you pray over a case, you are calling on God to attend to the case and that He will do at His own time. But when you speak to the case by reason of your faith in God, you will have your desired results – because the case will not wait for God to change but will respond to you directly- and that could even be instantly like in the case of Jairus' daughter.

Consider a scenario involving you and your father in a village. You are trying to sundry some foodstuff and there is this goat trying to eat the stuff. But instead of you driving it from the stuff, you start shouting, calling on your father who is probably in the farm (away from your location) to come and drive the goat away. That's what you do in prayers. Your father will surely answer you; and when he comes, he will only say 'kai' (the language used in some parts of Africa to scare animals like goats away) and the goat will go. Whereas if you had said the same 'kai', the goat would still have gone. So, most of the things we are praying and crying to God about could simply be solved by our 'speaking' –based on our faith in God. This means you don't have to bother waking Jesus up every time a storm arises; you too can say the same 'Peace be still' and the wind will obey you. Tell the devil 'kai' and the voice he will hear will be your Father's – because faith makes you sound like God. In Mark 11:23, Jesus said 'whosoever shall say to this mountain' not whosoever shall pray to God concerning this mountain. Prayer is reporting a case to God (not in a commanding tone) to be addressed by Him. But when you speak in faith, you are addressing the situation by yourself on behalf of God because your faith has put you in the capacity of God –and the results are usually the same. The case will be addressed because 'with God' and 'to him that believes', all things are possible. (Matthew 19:26c, Mark 9:23).

Action:

Call every situation or circumstance you come across by the name you want it to bear, and not necessarily by the name it already bears or what others call it. For instance, what doctors call 'fibroid' you can all 'fine boy', and according to the Mark 11:23, you will have it so. Remember, the moment Adam gave names to certain animals God created; they started bearing those names. Even God didn't edit the name – Genesis 2:19.

#Fourteen

Deuteronomy 2:36c [TLB]

'Not one city was too strong for us, for the Lord our God gave all of them to us'.

Application:
Until God gives you a thing, you surely can't have it. John 3:27 says "...a man can receive nothing, except it be given him from heaven". And if it is God Who is giving you anything, you won't need to struggle to have it. But when you begin to struggle to have or accomplish something, check it; maybe you are trying to have what the Lord your God has not given to you.

Action:
The best place to discover the 'cities' the Lord wants you to possess is the Bible. Dig out the promises of God for your life as contained in the scriptures and begin to lay claim on them; not one of them will be too strong for you to obtain because it is God Who gave all of them to you – Joshua 21:45, 1 Kings 8:56.

#Fifteen

Psalm 47:7 [AKJV]

'For God is the king of all the earth; sing ye praises with understanding'

Application:

Praise is a three-dimensional kingdom force available to every believer. Whenever praise is being offered to God, it takes care of the past, the present and the future – all of which attracts Divine Presence.

- Praising God for what He had already done (Past) – this is otherwise referred to as Reflective Praise; when one thinks on what God has done in the past. For example, in Exodus 15:1-21, Moses and the entire nation of Israel thought about their deliverance from Pharaoh and his hosts, and decided to give God praise. Hannah also remembered how the God of Israel had taken away her reproach of barrenness and she gave Him praise according to 1 Samuel 2:1-10.
Benefit – the testimony becomes PERMANENT!

- Praising God in the 'Now' (Present) – this is called Active Praise; that is, praising God in one's present situation, even when it is not convenient.
Jehoshaphat and the people of Judah practiced this in 2 Chron-

icles 20:1-30. They were faced with a life-threatening situation but still praised God. Also, Paul and Silas engaged in this active praise according to Acts 16:25-31 and God was pleased with them.
Benefit – God comes down right on the scene and intervenes.

- Praising God for your expectations (Future) – this is otherwise called Faith-Based or Focused Praise. Here, one praises God for He is yet to do but surely going to do. It is faith-based because though you can't see it yet, you are so convinced that it will be done; so you give praise in advance for it. This is the type that pleases God most because it proves to Him that one really believes and trusts in Him. It is anchored on the integrity of God and His infallible nature. For example, Abraham gave praises to God while He was still waiting for his son Isaac to be born – Romans 4:17-20. Everything looked like it was not possible but he focused his praise on his expectation not on his condition (experience) at the moment. Also, before Jesus raised Lazarus back to life in John 11: 41-44, He first gave praise for his resurrection. He praised God for what He expected to happen as if it had already happened. In summary, as long as your praises are directed to God regardless of the dimension you are engaging, He is committed to respond because He actually inhabits (dwells)in the praises of His people (Psalm 22:3).**Benefit – God moves heaven and earth to ensure that expectation comes to pass.**

Action:

1 Thessalonians 5:18 says 'In everything give thanks, for this is the will of God for you in Christ Jesus'. So whether for past events, present situations or future expectations; give God praise. And because He moved in the cases earlier mentioned, He will move in your own case too. He is the Lord; He changeth not (Malachi 3:6). Start praising God with understanding!

#Sixteen

Luke 8:46 [AKJV]

'And Jesus said, Somebody hath touched me; for I perceive that virtue is gone out of me'.

Application:
"Whenever a man touches God, virtues are released in his direction". When you touch Him, you receive your desired (purposed and expected) miracle(s).

Analyzing this statement reveals a lot. Firstly, Jesus said 'Somebody hath touched me' –not an Apostle, Prophet, Evangelist, Pastor, Deacon or Deaconess – hath touched me. He said 'somebody'; and somebody could actually be anybody. You don't need a spiritual pedigree or church title to be able or to qualify to touch Jesus. Anyone who can find their way to Jesus can touch Him – He is no respecter of persons (Rom 2:11; 1 Peter 1:17).

In our text, so many apostles and disciples had contact with Jesus, but it was only a stinking, despised and afflicted woman with 12 years issue of blood who really TOUCHED Him. And that means you too can touch Him –Praise God!

Secondly, it is important to consider how this woman touched Jesus. She only touched the hem (border) of His garment and Jesus termed it as 'touched me'. Verses 27 and 28 of Mark 5 say 'she had said if I may but touch His clothes, I shall be made whole'. So, she touched Jesus by FAITH (she believed, confessed and acted correspondingly). Jesus confirmed this in Luke 8:48 when He said 'her faith' (with which she touched Him) had made her whole.

To touch Jesus, you need faith (based on a particular preconceived expectation or something you hope for). The virtue that left Jesus left Him to do something somebody with faith was expecting; thus without an expectation or a particular well defined desire, you can't exercise faith. And as such, you can't be able to touch Him to attract virtues. At best, you will just be like others thronging Him without any miracle or testimony to show for it - because they weren't expecting anything from Him.

Thirdly, notice that the woman pressed in from behind to touch Jesus – Mark 5:27. There were multitudes following Jesus, but she broke through all oppositions, obstacles, and hindrances to touch Him. When she did, she got her miracle. The operation of faith is a fight. It involves 'pressing' (1 Timothy 6:12). "When your expectation or hope is established; and you have started exercising faith towards achieving it, there will be oppositions and obstacles which will make it look as if what you are hoping for will not happen. They are clear evidences or facts pointing towards the seemingly impossibility of getting your expectations fulfilled.

At this point, you need to 'press in'; you need to fight, you need to break your way through – like the men in Mark 2:2-5. You need to engage all the Word of God at your disposal, as well as the promises, prophecies and every other thing like relevant books, CDs etc you can lay your hands on so as to ensure you remain steadfast until that expectation is met. To have your 'issue of blood' dried up, be ready to press through the multitude (of oppositions and obstacles) to get to Jesus.

Lastly, the woman testified openly what the Lord had done for her; and her miracle was sealed. Whenever your expected miracle is delivered to you, learn to testify (openly) of His goodness. That way, He will be glorified, your miracle will be sealed (made secure) and others' faith will be enhanced to receive same manifestations in their own lives too. In Mark 6:56, when others heard her testimony, they came, touched Jesus' garment and were all made whole as well.

Action:

Every miracle recorded in scriptures can be repeated in your life if you dare to take the same steps the recipients of such miracles took. Believe, confess and act out your faith – your testimonies are inevitable.

#Seventeen

James 2:17, 26 [AKJV]

'Even so faith, if it hath not works, is dead, being alone. For as the body without the spirit is dead, so faith without works is dead also'.

Application:

1. Starting a vehicle and driving it without any particular destination in mind is an exercise in futility. In the same way, exercising faith without any expectation or established hope (which could be through a prophecy, promise or discovered truth in the scripture) is an exercise in futility.
2. Also, having a destination in mind without taking steps towards it is senseless. In like manner, expecting or hoping for something without taking steps of faith to achieve it is an exercise in futility. Such hope will never be released.
3. Furthermore, taking wrong steps towards an established destination will never lead there. In the same way, taking wrong steps and engaging wrong means to achieve a hope or expectation will never lead to the realization of that hope.

Mathematically, these three principles can be represented thus;

1. $A + B = C$
   Where A = Faith
   B = Action (right action)

C = Fulfilled Expectation (already preconceived while exercising faith and action).

Without 'C' – an expected result, there is no point engaging 'A' (faith) and 'B' (action).

2. $A + - \neq C$

Where A = Faith

- = No Action

C = Desired Result

Without 'B' (action), 'A' (faith) alone will never result in 'C' (desired result), because it takes A and B to produce 'C'.

1. $A + D \neq C$

Where A = Faith
B = Wrong Action
C = Desired Result

With 'D' (wrong action), your 'A' (faith) will never lead to 'C' (desired result) – because it takes the combination of 'A' and 'B' to produce 'C'.

Note however that 'D' is also an action, but it is not the right action (B) that is needed to produce 'C'.

If you need a good child for instance, and you decide to combine visiting a native doctor with your faith; you won't have your desired result – a good child. The native doctor may through his diabolical means 'help' you conceive, but such a child will be a counterfeit 'C' – one that may grow up to torment you for the rest of your life because it's from the devil. And that's not your desire.

Let's consider one more equation;

- $- + B \neq C$

Where $-$ = Doubt (faithlessness, unbelief)
B = Right Action
C = Desired Result

As a matter of fact, the output of such equation will be zero i.e. "$- + B = 0$" (no result from your expected Source – God). According to James 1:5-7, asking is a right action but without faith (A), your right actions are useless because they will never produce 'C' (your desired result). This is because it is only 'A' (faith) and 'B' (right action) that can generate 'C' (your desired result) – James 2:17, 26.

Action:

Have faith in God, take corresponding (right) actions and you will have your desired results. This formula works for all God's children. If you are one, then you can start applying it – John 13:17.

#Eighteen

Psalm 119: 144b [AKJV]

'...give me understanding and I shall live'.

Application:
Understanding is directly proportional to living. That is, if anyone is ever interested in living, what he should go for is understanding. Conversely, anyone who is lacking in understanding is not permitted to live because the required ingredient for living is not found in him – Proverbs 21:16. Not going in the way of understanding is foolishness, and the end product is DEATH – Proverbs 9:6.

One major advantage of understanding is that it makes you live, and not merely exist. To live means to fulfill your purpose in life, to enjoy health, wealth, relationship, prosperity etc. All that makes life worth living are yours the moment you get understanding.

Note that the Psalmist did not say 'give me anointing and I shall live', neither did he say 'give me money, health, power, influence, connections etc and I shall live'. Rather, he said 'give me understanding and I shall live'. This is because he knew the moment God gives him understanding, every other thing he needs to live a fulfilled life will be automatically released to him even without necessarily asking for them. Understanding is like the key to a house with many rooms filled with untold treasures- 1 Kings 3:1-14 (emphasis on verses 9-13) and chapter 4:29-34.

Proverbs 21:16 presents the danger of lack of understanding. It says the man who wanders from the way of understanding shall remain (rest) in the congregation of the dead. So, it is very dangerous to be void of understanding.

The scriptures give examples of some categories of people who are referred to as fools because of lack of understanding;

1. An adulterer lacks understanding; he's an utter fool – Proverbs 6:32 (KJV/TLB).
2. An anxious fellow (whose spirit is not calm) lacks understanding – Proverbs 17:27.
3. Someone who says in his heart that there is no God – Psalm 14:1
4. Anyone who disobeys God lacks understanding – Proverbs 2:6b

These are just to mention a few.

The scriptures also present God as the Source of understanding – through His Word and His Spirit;

1. Proverbs 2:6b – from His mouth cometh knowledge and understanding.
2. Psalm 119:144b – (God) give me understanding...
3. 1 Kings 3:12; 4:29 – God gave Solomon understanding...
4. Luke 24:45 – Jesus opened their understanding that they might comprehend the scriptures (through His Word) – Psalm 119:130.
5. Hebrews 11:3 – by faith in God, we understand...
6. Job 32:8 – 'But there is a spirit in man, and the inspiration (breath) of the Almighty gives him understanding (through the Holy Spirit).

What then is understanding? Proverbs 9:10b says 'And the knowledge of the Holy One (God) is understanding' (KJV). The Living Bible Translation says 'Knowing God results in every other kind of understanding'.

- To have understanding in the area of justice, what knowledge of God do you have as pertaining to justice?
- To have understanding in the area of marriage, what knowledge of God do you possess as pertaining to marriage?

In order to receive understanding from God (the Source), you will have to get His Words – look at them, read them, hear them, listen to them, meditate on them and ask His Holy Spirit to quicken your understanding and enlarge your heart for divine release of inspiration –stay focused on that word (knowledge) you want to understand; as you do this, the light of revelation will start shining in your heart and in no time, you will be will be enlightened inwardly (in your inner man).

As this begins to happen, pick your pen or iPad (or any other writing material) and start documenting all your revelations pertaining to the matter. Think more, search more, observe and reason the more, you may still see some other things.

Upon getting this illumination, you need to check how it affects you and take steps of action right away – either by imbibing the principle learned into your daily living or carrying out certain discovered instructions. Just do whatever the Holy Spirit tells you to do –John 2:5.

It is also important to note that different types of understanding exist; yet from the same Source – God.

1. Understanding of justice (a discerning heart) – 1 Kings 3:9-11
2. Understanding of the times (knowing what ought to be done per time) -1 Chronicles 12:32
3. Understanding of the scriptures (ability to fully comprehend the meaning of scriptural truths and principles) – Luke 24:25, Daniel 9:2
4. Understanding of visions and dreams – Daniel 1:17
5. Understanding of all mysteries and all knowledge – 1 Corinthians 13:2, Luke 8:10-11

6. Understanding of the will of God – Ephesians 5:17

Action:

Solomon prayed for an understanding heart and he was given. Pray for it as well and you shall be given –Matthew 7:7.

#Nineteen

1 Corinthians 3: 21-23, John 20:21-23

'...all things are yours...'
1 Corinthians 6: 16-17, John 20: 17b
'...he that is joined unto the Lord is one spirit...'

Application:
The first scripture says 'all things are mine – life, death, the world, the present, and the future' because I'm Christ's and Christ is God's.

Relating this to verse 17 of 1 Corinthians 6 which says once I give my life to Christ, God starts seeing me the same way He sees Christ; it therefore implies that because I'm born again, God looks at me, sees me, relates with me, talks with me, identifies with me etc the same way He does with His Son –Jesus Christ.

As a result of this, if God answers Jesus' prayers, He definitely answers mine too. If He sees Jesus as righteous, then He sees me as righteous too. If He sees Jesus as perfect, then I am perfect in His sight. If He doesn't see any sin in Jesus, He doesn't see any in me as well. He loves me the same way He loves Jesus and because He has committed all things into Jesus' Hands, He has done same to me- Colossians 1:15-23. That's why all things are mine. That means whatever responds to Jesus must respond to me because I'm the Jesus on earth now by His commission and mandate (1 John 4:17b).

Whatever cannot befall Jesus cannot befall me. I'm enjoying the same immunity with Christ. The whole of God has been poured into Christ; thus I also have all of God in me. And according to Revelation 5:10 and Revelation 1:6, He (Christ) hath made me a king and priest unto God; and I'm to reign on earth. Meaning my domain is the earth as declared by Christ Jesus. So, He has given me all the earth for my own discretional use. The whole earth is my sphere of influence – Psalm 115:16. Everyone and everything on this earth must respond to my command. Where the word of a king is, there is power –Ecclesiastes 8:4. Little wonder He says in the first scripture that the world (earth) is for my use. I can effect any change I think necessary on the earth – either at home or abroad. I can kill and give life because death and life are my servants. Christ Jesus is indestructible and as such I'm an indestructible entity. Also, Christ is the Head of all principalities and I, being a member of His Body, inseparably joined together with Him also have power over principalities, powers, witches, wizards, forces of darkness etc. They must respect me because they respect Jesus.

Action:
If you believe this is so, start living like it is so and it shall surely be so.

#Twenty

Psalm 119:89

'Forever Oh Lord, thy Word is settled in heaven'
'Your word stands firm in heaven' (TLB)
Note also Genesis 15:1-end (Emphasis on verses 4-6); Jeremiah 29:4-14.

Application:
There is nothing God is saying He will do now that He hasn't already done in Heaven. Every of His promises to you is already existing in the heavenly realm, they are only awaiting 'an appointed time' or 'due season' or 'certain time of life' to manifest in the physical.

Not seeing them happen now doesn't mean they are not yours; they are surely yours. Just that the time for their manifestation is not ripe yet – according to God's plan. He alone knows what He's doing and why He's doing it. 'Only believe Me' is His commandment to you. If you believe Him, there will be performance of those things He has promised you – Luke 1:45.

Consider these case studies;

1. Jeremiah 1:1-12 (emphasis on verses 4-7) – Read it please.
   In Jeremiah's file with God, he existed as a prophet and not as a child even though he saw himself as a child. But God had to change his orientation, and in verse 12, he started seeing as God sees.
2. Abraham had always existed before God as a father of many nations, and God saw him that way. But physically he was child-

less as it were. However, God helped him to see what was in his file by showing him the innumerable stars of heaven. On seeing them, he believed and when God was ready, He gave him the promise –Isaac.
3. Moses and the Ark of the Covenant's description. God gave Moses dimensions according to the pattern (of the heavenly one) showed to him.
4. Joseph was already a Prime Minister of Egypt before he was born.
5. Jesus went to the heavenly Holy of holies to make atonement for our sins. Not the earthly one – being attended to by the High Priest because that was just a shadow of the real heavenly one –Hebrews 9: 23-25.

Nothing will manifest on earth that has not already existed (settled /stood firm) in heaven.

Your own responsibility is just to believe His promises to you; trust Him, follow His instructions, obey Him totally and you will surely see His Word manifest in your own very life.

Ecclesiastes 3:11 says He hath made everything beautiful in his time (not your own time).

Isaiah 55:8-9 says His ways are not your ways. Consider this scenario; the Board of Directors of a particular organization had a meeting and decided to increase the salary of their workers at a particular period of the year. Although this has been settled, the workers (who are not aware of the details of the Directors' meeting) will have to keep on working, trusting and waiting until there is implementation. That's how it is with 'waiting on God'.

Action:
Don't stop trusting. If He has promised it, He will surely fulfill it – Numbers 23:19, Genesis 21:1.

#Twenty One

Psalm 139:14

'I will praise thee for I am fearfully and wonderfully made; marvelous are thy works and that my soul knoweth right well'.

Application:
To be 'wonderful' means to be full of wonders (amazement), while to be 'fearful' means to be full of fears (dread). It therefore follows that as a Christian (child of God), you are full of wonders and at the same time full of dread. That is, to some people you are wonderful, while to some others you are dreadful (fearsome).

When in contact with the godly (God's children), you are wonderful and pleasant to be with. But when in contact with the wicked (the ungodly), you are a horror to them, so dreadful and fearsome to be with. Thus, it is where one in contact with you belongs that will tell whether it will be wonderful being with you or dreadful. 2 Corinthians 2:16 says to the one we are the savour of death unto death; and to the other the savour of life unto life.

Action:
Maintain your relationship with God and don't accommodate sin. If you do, your presence will bring salvation to those in need of it and judgment to those deserving it.

Become a Financial Partner with Jesus

At *Global Emancipation Ministries - Calgary*, our mandate is *to liberate men through the knowledge of the Truth* and our mission statement is *creating channels through which men can encounter the Truth [Isaiah 61:1-3; John 8:32, 36; I Thessalonians 5:24].*

Our Ministerial Activities include Rural and Urban Evangelical Outreaches, Prison Evangelism, Hospital Ministrations, Mobilization for Missions Support, Teaching of the undiluted Word of God, Scripture-Based Seminars, Discipleship, Training of Field Missionaries and Empowerment of underprivileged ones among other Field Ministerial Tasks.

If you sense the Lord is calling you to reach out to the lost by engaging in any of these activities or by assisting those involved with your resources, please feel free to join us. Let us come together as we take the Gospel of our Lord Jesus Christ to the hurting and forgotten ones.

[Mark 16:15-20].

Please join us in these kingdom projects by making your weekly, monthly, quarterly or annual donations to Global Emancipation Ministries – Calgary.

You can visit the "GIVE" section on our website, www.gloem.org, to learn about other ways to give.

For acknowledgement, please advise your donations to us by email: info@gloem.org or emancipation4souls@yahoo.com, and kindly include your details i.e. name, address, email and location. Alternatively, you can simply call +1 587 9735910 to do same.

You can also volunteer your gifts and talents in the service of the Lord through our ministerial platforms regardless of your location. To get information on how to go about this, please visit www.gloem.org and contact us via email: info@gloem.org or emancipation4souls@yahoo.com.

God bless you.

About the Author

By the special grace of God, **Anthony O. Adefarakan** is the privileged President of **Global Emancipation Ministries - Calgary (GLOEM)** with headquarters in Canada, North America and **Emancipating Truth Ministry International (ETMI)** with headquarters in Nigeria, West Africa.

The Lord called him into the field ministry in February 2008 with the mandate to liberate men through the knowledge of the Truth, and by December 2012 he was ordained and commissioned as the Pioneer Pastor – in – Charge of The Redeemed Christian Church of God, Revelation Parish, Shalom Area under Delta Province III, Nigeria where he served until 1st February 2015 when he officially handed over to a new Pastor in order to focus on his field ministry to which the Lord had earlier called him and for which the authority of the church had already prayed and released him to undertake.

On 29th September 2013, he was awarded a Post Graduate Diploma in Tent – Making Mission from the Redeemed Christian School of Missions, Nigeria (RECSOM, Asaba Campus) where he also had the privilege to train Pastors and Missionaries as a lecturer in 2017.

Since the commissioning of his field ministry in 2015 he has had the opportunity to lead his ministry officers to field ministrations in different Prisons, Hospitals, Orphanages, Rural communities, Camp settlements, Markets, Local churches among other places with great successes on all occasions – such as salvation of sinners, healing of the sick, financial empowerment of mission churches, provision of relief materials to the poor, provision of medical services to the underprivileged, baptism in the Holy Ghost, deliverance from demonic oppression, release of inmates just to mention a few - all to the glory of God Who alone is the Doer.

He is the author of other best-selling titles such as *Learning from the Ants, It's Your Size, The Immutability of God's Counsel, Surely there is an End, Life Applicable lessons from the Book of Ruth, The Law of Kinds, One thing is Needful , Life Applicable Revelations from God's Word* among others.

He is happily married to Ifeoluwa A. Adefarakan and their marriage is fruitful to the glory of God.

Jesus is his Message, Freedom is the Outcome!
Isaiah 61:1-3

www.ingramcontent.com/pod-product-compliance
Lightning Source LLC
Chambersburg PA
CBHW071915070526
44583CB00016B/1998